Green and Spiky

What Am I?

by Joyce Markovics

Consultant: Eric Darton, Adjunct Faculty
New York University Urban Design and Architecture Studies Program
New York, New York

New York, New York

Credits

Cover, © Katharina M/Shutterstock; 2, © evenfh/Shutterstock; TOC, © Karl R. Martin/Shutterstock; 4–5, © luca amedei/Shutterstock; 6–7, © Karl R. Martin/Shutterstock; 8–9, © Rubens Alarcon/Shutterstock; 10–11, © Mikhail Leonov/Shutterstock; 12–13, © Chris Parypa Photography/Shutterstock; 14–15, © evenfh/Shutterstock; 16–17, © evenfh/Shutterstock; 18–19, © Andrius K/Shutterstock; 20–21, © Andrius K/Shutterstock; 22–23, © Luciano Mortula-LGM/Shutterstock; 24, © Sviluppo/Shutterstock.

Publisher: Kenn Goin
Senior Editor: Joyce Tavolacci
Creative Director: Spencer Brinker
Design: Debrah Kaiser
Photo Researcher: Thomas Persano

Library of Congress Cataloging-in-Publication Data in process at time of publication (2018)
Library of Congress Control Number: 2017039494
ISBN-13: 978-1-68402-478-0

For more information, write to Bearport Publishing Company, Inc., 45 West 21st Street, Suite 3B, New York, New York 10010. Printed in the United States of America.

10 9 8 7 6 5 4 3 2 1

Contents

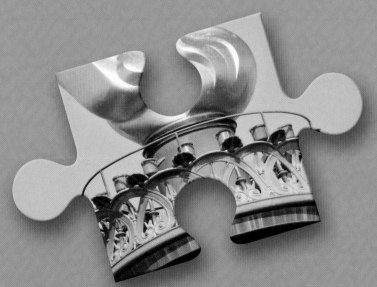

What Am I?

Look at my huge
nose.

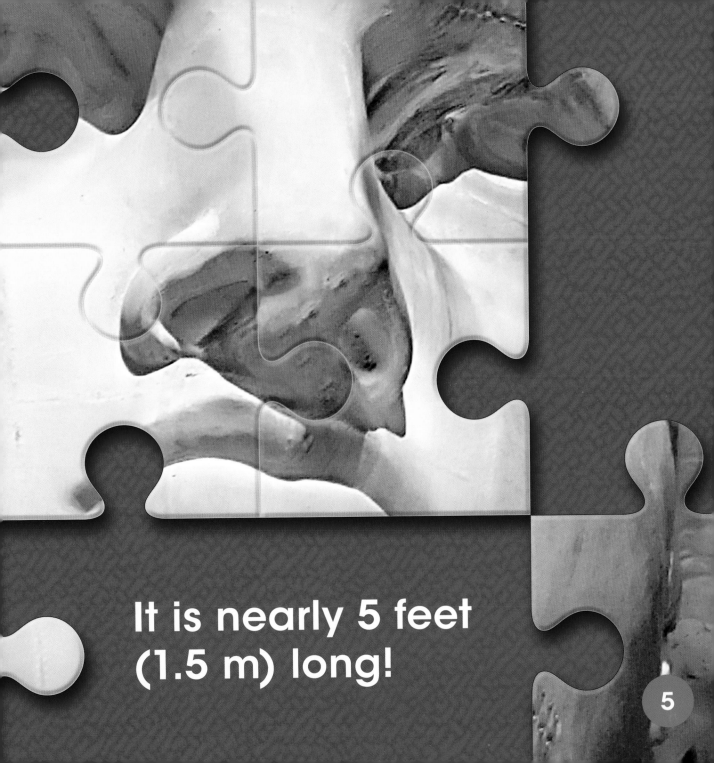

It is nearly 5 feet
(1.5 m) long!

6

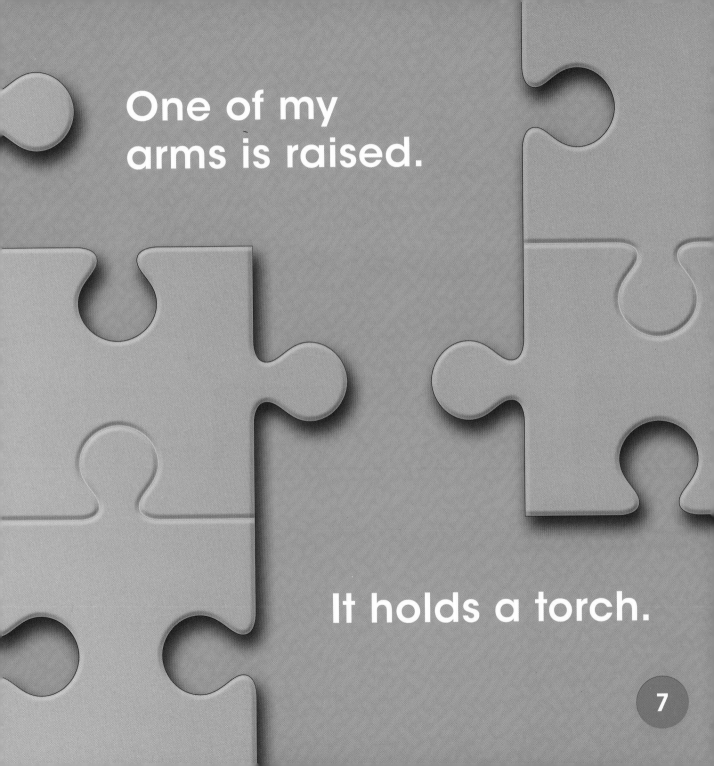

One of my
arms is raised.

It holds a torch.

I am covered in metal called copper.

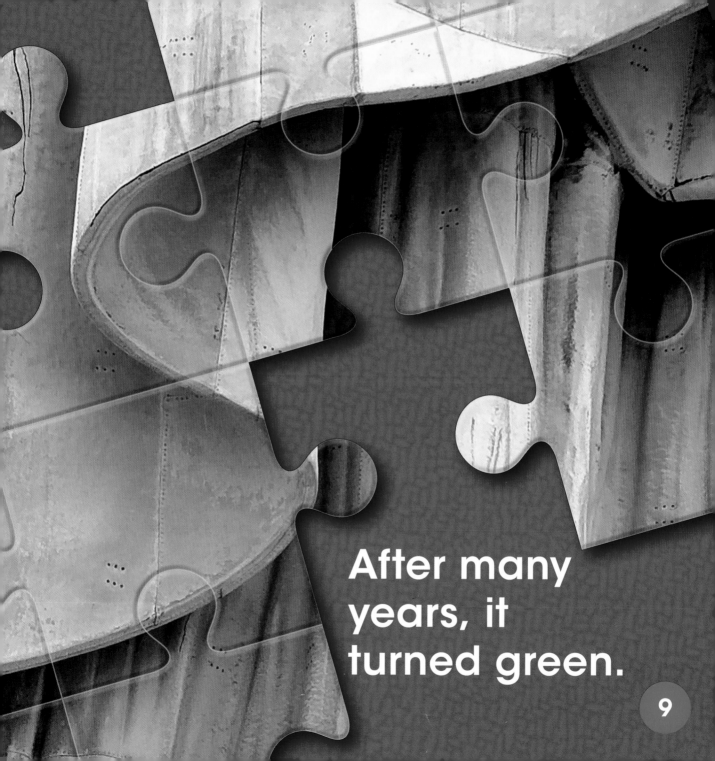

After many years, it turned green.

9

My base is stone
and concrete.

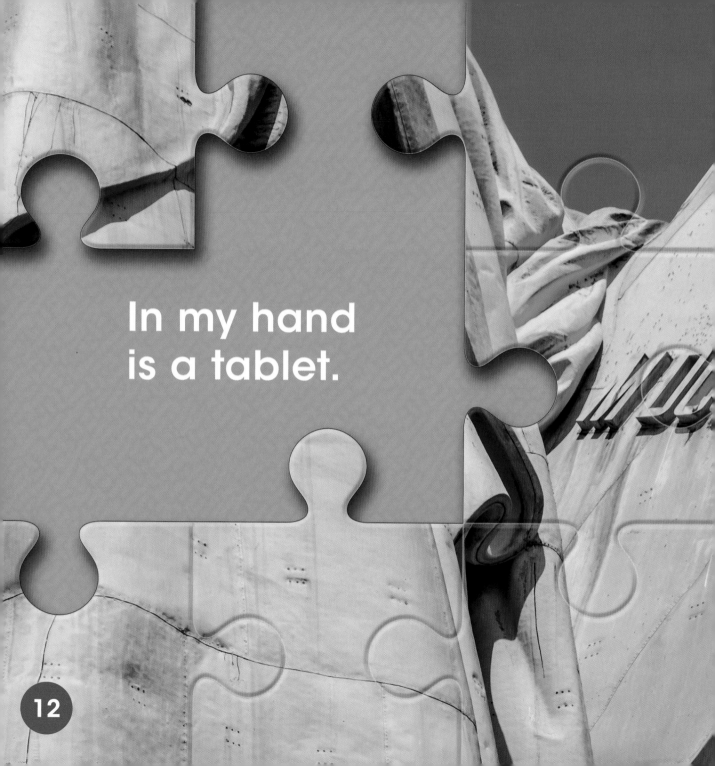

In my hand
is a tablet.

It says July 4,
1776—that's
Independence Day!

My crown
is green
and spiky.

It has seven
spikes.

A person has to climb 377 stairs to reach my crown.

16

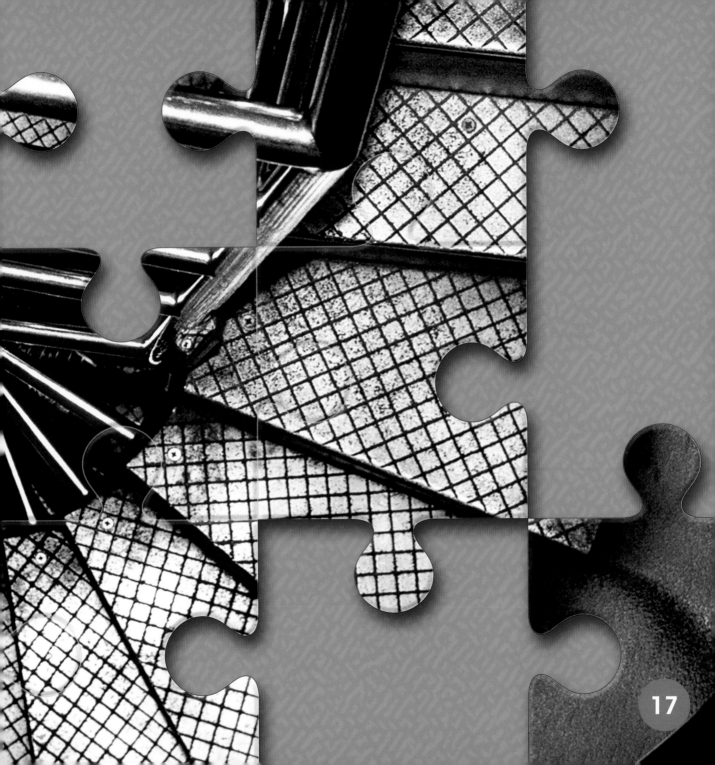

What am I?

Let's find out!

I am the Statue of Liberty!

21

Fast Facts

The Statue of Liberty was a gift from France in 1886. The statue is a symbol of freedom—and welcomes people from all over the world.

The Statue of Liberty

Total Height:	305 feet 6 inches (93 m) from the base to the torch
Weight:	450,000 pounds (204,117 kg)
Height of Head:	17 feet 3 inches (5.26 m)
Width of One Eye:	2 feet 6 inches (0.76 m)
Width of Mouth:	3 feet (0.9 m)
Length of Right Arm:	42 feet (12.8 m)
Cool Fact:	Each year, hundreds of bolts of lightning strike the statue.

Where Am I?

The Statue of Liberty stands on Liberty Island in New York Harbor near New York City.

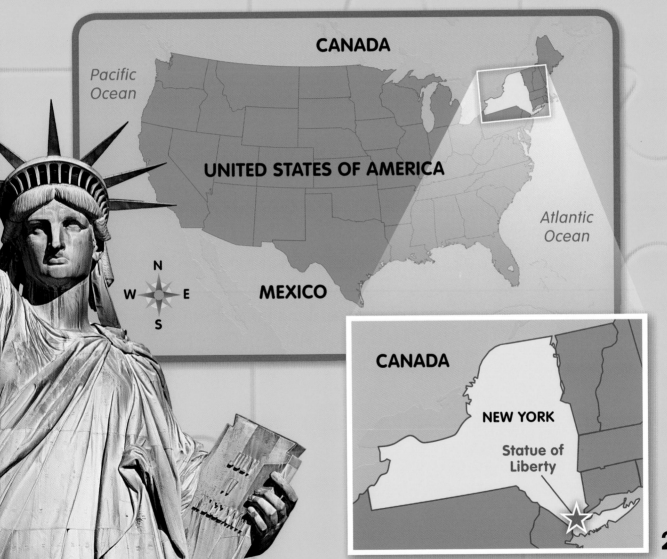

Index

Read More

Holub, Joan. *What Is the Statue of Liberty?* New York: Grosset & Dunlap (2014).

Penner, Lucille Recht. *The Statue of Liberty.* New York: Random House (1995).

Learn More Online

To learn more about the Statue of Liberty, visit
www.bearportpublishing.com/AmericanPlacePuzzlers

About the Author

Joyce Markovics is a proud New Yorker who lives in a very old house along the Hudson River. She marvels at the Statue of Liberty every time she sees it.